# Teaching

## *My Art*  *My Heart*

# Teaching

## My Art My Heart

IKE WILLIAMS

Editor : Antonio Smith
Email Address : antoniosmith242@gmail.com

Library of Congress Control Number:          2020903199

HARDBACK:            978-1-952155-19-2
PAPERBACK:           978-1-952155-18-5
EBOOK:               978-1-952155-20-8



Ordering Information:

For orders and inquiries, please contact:
1-888-404-1388
www.goldtouchpress.com
book.orders@goldtouchpress.com

Printed in the United States of America

In this work, I share the idea that sparked its publication, as well as the events that catapulted me into the teaching profession. I also share my philosophies, experiences, and the emotions I felt as a teacher through the course of my career.

*A short look into the window of a teacher's philosophy, feelings, and experiences.*

This book is dedicated to every single student I was blessed to teach and love, whether in a structured curricular institution or in an extra-curricular environment.

It is also dedicated to teachers who minister to young lives through the art of the educational profession.

"Jesus is the greatest teacher…if we teach, we should follow in His footsteps."

(Eisenhower. J. Williams)

# CONTENTS

# PREFACE

*There is a purpose for which we were born.*
*Finding that purpose is a journey, and an experience.*
*There are no bad experiences in life,*
*Especially for people who believe in Christ.*
*The Bible states that,*
*"All things work together for good for those who*
*Love the Lord, and are called according to His purpose."*
*Purpose is founded on tribulation,*
*and with tribulation comes experience.*
*Experience is multiplied and enriched on the journey.*

*In this work, I share the idea that sparked its publication, as well as the events that catapulted me into the teaching profession. I also share my philosophies, experiences, and the emotions I felt as a teacher through the course of my career.*

# 1

## The Beginning

Another day, mid–morning, the students were settled at their desks writing. I had just revised with them the elements of good story writing. They were now engaged in a writing exercise for more practice.

There was a fragile calm in the room which could be easily broken, even by a fly on the wall. I was glad for the peace. I tried to finish the reading report before me, hoping to meet the impending deadline. Deadlines frequently came from the office and, from my point of view, interrupted the joy of teaching.

"Sir, I am writing a story,"

A voice near my desk broke the calm.

"That is what you are supposed to be doing," I thought to myself. The voice came from Octavia, a smart Indian girl who had come from South Africa to live on the island. Some of the students in my class were natives, with parents who were natives. Others were natives, with one parent being a native and the other a foreigner. My students were from different nationalities, races, backgrounds and cultures.

"Can I read it?" I asked, not eagerly, as I really did not want to be disturbed, since I was pressed for time to get the reading evaluation before me done. It had to be in the office on time. Not meeting a deadline was a serious offence in this school.

"No sir!" she replied bubbly, "This is how far I've got," holding up two sheets of folder papers with writing on the four sides.

"You did all that in this short time?" I asked, sort of impressed.

"Yes sir, but I am not quite finished yet," she said in her gentle South African accent.

"Why don't we all try and write a story with a couple of chapters?" I suddenly blurted out. At the same time, I was trying to figure out in my head how to motivate the class, to embark upon this huge task. Knowing full well how reluctant some were, even to write a paragraph.

"You can use the next two terms to work on your stories," I said slowly. "I will read them and help with the corrections, then; we could publish them and have them on display, the day of your gradation from Grade Six."

A buzz of excitement flooded the room. Everyone began chatting together with positive responses to my idea.

"Are you going to write one too?" a voice asked piercing through the hum of the excitement.

"Why not?" came off my lips with uncertainty. I knew I already had too much on my plate. Why would I want to add writing a story to the list? However, the question still hung in the air and, as my students looked at me expectantly, it struck a chord somewhere deep within my soul.

Writing a book was something I'd always thought of doing, someday, if I ever got the time. Perhaps the time was now. Well, if accepting the challenge to write would stimulate the students' interest to do the same, then who was I to stand in the way of the inspiration welling up inside of them?

"Yes Neta, I will," I heard myself saying. Applause filled the room as the fire was lit.

"Cool!" she replied, "Will it be about us?" I laughed at the thought. "I am not sure."

One thing I knew, this was going to be a challenge I would not back down from. I was past the point of no return. The story had to be written, but where would I start? A thought floated up from my heart and into my mind. 'Whatever you write, it must come from the heart.'

# 2

## The Path

To become a teacher was no desire of mine. It was rather providential how the profession targeted me…

Looking back, I remember the vacant feelings.

I had finished high school, and felt like I had accomplished nothing. I felt lost and betrayed. I had no clue as to what I wanted to do with my life. The job I took as a library assistant was only to pass time, to give me something to do, to have my own money to spend. I was a free spirit with no agenda but to enjoy life.

Had I arrived at the place to decide upon a career, I think I would have opted to become a lawyer, a sociologist, or a historian, certainly not a teacher.

Working at the city library was dull. Excitement came only when I worked the front desk. There, I got the opportunity to chat up readers returning or checking out books. But, when assigned to the book room where books were repaired, sorted or re-shelved, it was only an exercise in mindless work. The only time I came alive during those sessions, was when I spotted a book that craved my attention, just begging to be read.

It was lunch time, on one of those days when I was assigned mindless work. My girlfriend visited the library and asked me to accompany her to an interview at a teacher's college two or three blocks away from the library. I was happy at the prospect of not having to go to the lunch room to sit with boring staff, who were older than me, and with whom I had nothing in common.

"Let's go," I said without hesitating. I was happy for the opportunity to be out in the fresh air. We strolled down the cool, tree lined avenue. I felt alive again, enjoying the vibrant colors of various flowers and shrubs that edged the sidewalk on the way to the college. The thought of where I would have lunch popped in my mind, but I told myself that I would detour through the crossroad section of the city on my way back to work and grab something to eat from one of the many food vendors who were sprinkled in the area.

It was my first time setting foot on the grounds of this noble institution. The City's Teachers' College. Suddenly, a strange and unexpected wave of excitement rippled through my body and gave me goose bumps. I felt compelled to investigate the source of this oddly spontaneous sensation. While my girlfriend went to her interview, I wandered the campus freely, and acquainted myself with the unknown territory.

As I perused through groups of seemingly nervous and excited candidates waiting at different departments to be called for their interviews, I wondered what was going through their heads.

I continued my unguided tour, taking in the unfamiliar sights, until I found myself curiously and cautiously peeping through the doorway of a room on the second floor of the English Department. I was puzzled as to why there were no students crowded here as they were at other places.

"Are you here for an interview?" a female voice from the interior of the dimly lit room came at me. As my eyes adjusted to the changes from coming out of the strong sunlight, I saw three starchy, well dressed ladies sitting at a table at the front of the room. One was white, one half white, and one black.

"No," I said unsure of myself, trying to keep the surprise out of my voice.

"Come in anyway," one said.

"Sit down and read this passage."

I was handed a sheet of paper with a selection. I was curious as to why on earth I was asked to read, when I distinctly said I was not there to be interviewed. Well, what the heck? I decided to read, and read I did, with my most dramatic theatrical voice, based on my experience of reading so many Shakespeare plays in school, and from my involvement with a local community theater group in the town where I lived.

"Young man!" exclaimed one of the ladies when I was through. "You are the best reader we have had all morning, take these forms down to the administrative office and register to attend this college."

And so it happened. Was this my destiny, my purpose? Everything in my life had brought me to this place. Should I walk away or accept?

# 3

## My Philosophy

The first term was almost at an end. The Christmas holidays were on the way. Only two terms left in the school year. Ahead, my students had to be prepared to sit two big exams near the end of the school year. I was more bothered by these exams than they were. Students' success in exams was a yard stick used by this education system to determine how good a teacher was. For me, the irritation was that the curriculum was much too focused on examination results and not focused enough on purpose and children's individual talents.

My belief is that education today is not as appealing to the present generation as it was when I was a child. Education, I believe, has lost its strong pull as a means of mobility; at least as it was for me and the poor people

I grew up around. It is now in competition with drugs, popular culture, and the rise in technology.

Growing up, education for me and those like me was a way out, the pathway to a better life. At least that's what our parents drummed in our heads. It was the stuff dreams were made of. Not so today!

I fear today that my students are far more distracted by the technology and gadgets they have at their disposal. They consume too much television, computer, internet, cell phone, and electronic games. And the list will become longer as humanity advances. Students are often allowed to have all these things because that is how some parents make up for the absence of quality time shared with their child.

The art of oral reading and spelling too, are systematically destroyed by some of these toys. The heart of any loving teacher bleeds at the devastation that is gnawing at the roots of traditional values and practices. What is to be done? Do I just sit back and watch? No! I have to make it work; I must find ways and means to draw my students back into a world of value and wonder through education.

Back to a place where drug dealers, movie stars, sport stars and rap artists are not their sole idols; back to the place where school is not a boring ordeal, back to the place where they wake up with excitement to attend school.

I sometimes spend nights wondering about my students. Why did this one or that one not understand this or that concept?

How can this be re-taught in a fun or simpler way?

Does he or she have a learning problem?

What can I do to help?

I cannot go on if my students are not learning. I see their faces and wonder about their future. They are individuals in their own rights, unique, with a purpose placed inside them by the creator God.

What will they become later in life? Am I building the right foundation for each one?

Questions, questions, questions, "There are more questions than answers" the saying goes.

As a teacher, I want to be sure that I am impactful; a positive influence on young lives, not just for the year they spend with me in a particular grade. I want to know that I am able to plant a seed that will bear good fruits in the future. Whatever I give, or impart, I want it to be true. I want it to be valuable. I want it to be precious. Something they can hold on to. Something they can draw upon when the journey of life becomes difficult. I don't want to teach from the outside in, I want to teach from the inside out.

*"It is not what goes into a man that defiles him,*
*It is what comes out"*

Education is about sowing seeds. Seeds of knowledge mixed in with the seeds of love, especially the love of God.

*'The fear of God is the beginning of all wisdom'*

Not fear in the sense of being afraid, but fear in the understanding of the awesome respect that is due to God for what He offers us.

I want my teaching to touch the hearts of my students. Awaken an inward desire for learning within them. By this, an insight of their true talents and abilities will be realized. Thus, destiny and purpose will be found.

For this to be accomplished, children must truly be educated in the admonishment of the fear of God. No true wisdom, knowledge, and understanding can be attained unless the seeds are planted in God.

*'Train up a child the way they should go...'*

In order to do that, one must be able to discern from early on, based on the gifts and talents within, where the child might be heading and nurture that. In my thinking one of the golden rules of education is helping students find purpose; their purpose.

Many students who have the luxury and good fortune of a standard education, in a formal and conducive atmosphere, are not aware of how blessed they are in comparison to the millions of children worldwide, who are deprived of this basic children's right.

The privileged must be taught not to take their education lightly. They must know that they are not just being educated for themselves; their education is for the world.

A thing of great value is lost to the world if students are not educated from early to understand and find purpose; however, purpose must be based on the concept of training up a child in the way that they should go. That is true purpose!

As a teacher, I try to identify as early as possible, the potentials, latent or obvious, in each individual child I teach. Teaching, therefore, cannot just be a collective operation; it also has to be very individualistic in nature.

Contrary to what some may believe, no one comes into this world by accident. Everyone is unique, so unique in fact that no two persons have the same finger prints, which tells me that we are each here for a specific reason.

Consider this, you came in this world to be a writer, but lived and died without accomplishing that purpose. One might shrug it off as 'no big thing'; however, the fact of the matter is that no one else could have written as you would have. Your style, your unique approach, your individualism would not have been matched by any other human. Your writing is lost to the world. I cringe when I think, when I contemplate on how much has been lost to humanity because of people who were not afforded the opportunity to fulfill their purpose. They lived and died, and their purpose was never stirred in them. What a loss!

A purpose driven life is a very rewarding way to live. If we neglect our purpose, we merely exist.

One important truth I have discovered in all my years of teaching, which stands out among many others, is that if you create opportunities for students to laugh while they are learning, they will learn more and forget less. In other words, if students are happy learners, more will stick in their minds.

My students are special to me. I try to make them happy. Each is like equipment that comes with a manual on how it is to be assembled, however students don't come with manuals. As a teacher it is my job to learn how to assemble each individual as best I can. To transform them into the best that they can be.

The school system expects them to be successful in exams but I have to do more than that. I have to ensure that I am building a foundation on which they can stand for life. As I interact with each child throughout the year, I have to find out what is missing. What is broken? What is defective? What is needed? I must strive to find the best learning strategy for each child. I have to guide them toward finding true purpose.

No two children are the same. Therefore, the traditional generalized approach in teaching must be blended with individualized instruction in careful and skillful ways. This is a difficult balancing act, and often a source of frustration.

Teaching is physically, physiologically, and emotionally draining. But, the joy of seeing the spark in a child's eyes when the light goes on is priceless!

# 4

## Class Time

"**Pling!**" The sound signal I make with my voice to get students' attention… **"e-mail from God"** twenty-five voices chimed in chorus in response to the familiar signal. That is how my class begins in the mornings, at least for the three days of the week when my students' first class begins with me.

*'e-Mail from God'*, is a book that I will read to students for the rest of my life, so long as I am able to teach. This book was a gift from a colleague, a former kindergarten teacher. It is a book that turned out to be a blessing to my students and me. This is a book that keeps on giving I would say. The one page daily readings are motivational, inspirational, and spiritual. It is in the form of an e-mail letter from God. It is super! In it, the writer deals with all

kinds of topics relevant to kids. It is as if God is speaking to them personally.

Following the reading I have a prayer, a song and the reciting of a psalm or scripture verses. The scriptures are given to students to study on a weekly basis. All these activities are done after the morning announcements, school prayer, national anthem and pledge of allegiance which comes from the office into the class via the intercom. The e-mail from God selection settles the students and they begin the day on a positive note.

The prayer I taught my students to recite in the mornings is a favorite childhood prayer of mine that my mother taught me. I have passed this on as a gift to my students.

*'I have wake and seen the light God has kept*
*me through the night Make me good oh Lord I*
*pray And keep and guide me through this day.'*
*Amen!*

It is amazing how childhood memories and experiences can shape our lives. Maybe this is a way that I honor my mother's memory, because each time this prayer is prayed by my students, my mother lives on in my heart.

The song following the prayer was taught to me by a Grade Three student of mine many years ago at another school where I taught. I can still see the joy on that little black face when I asked her to teach me and the rest of the class her song. She just started singing her song out of the blue after she had prayed my mother's prayer.

*'Thank you for waking me up this morning
Thank you for starting me on my way Thank
you for just allowing me to see another day.'*

"Blow me down," I thought when I heard her song, what a fitting complement to my mother's prayer. I felt the song was too short; it ended too quickly so I made up another verse.

*'Thank you for all the trees and flowers
Thank you for all the birds that sing
Thank you for just allowing me to see
another day.'*

Every year since then, I would not only teach my childhood prayer to my new class at the beginning of every school year, but also the song that child taught me. Both prayer and song, I felt, went together like hand in glove. These two gifts I pass on consistently. Actually, education is about passing on, passing on knowledge, passing on values, passing on culture, dreams and whatever else one wishes to pass on.

Class work begins, and in between teaching, there is disciplining and keeping students focused…

The class is becoming too noisy!

**"High Five!"** I belt out in a strong voice. The students responded in chorus.

**"*Eyes on speaker
Be quiet
Hands folded
Listen.*"**

High Five is a disciplinary strategy used throughout the school to get students to pay attention when they become too talkative and are not listening. The moment a teacher spouts "High five" with palm held high in the air and fingers spread. Students would stop talking and repeat, "Eyes on speaker, be quiet, hands folded, listen," and for awhile everything would be under control.

This is a strategy that worked well in schools in another country. It was adopted by my school when some of our teachers and administrators, including myself, visited and attended a reading workshop there. The lesson continues…

"What color is this?"

"Blue"

"Blue? This is green; you are not paying attention, and think before you speak".

Moving on…

"The dog jumped over the fence. Did you hear what I just said?"

"Yes sir!' the class replied.

"Ok, you! What did I just say?"

"The dog sat on the fence"

"My word!"…

I go ballistic. "Boy, you heard me say that?"

Listening is a skill to be taught. It is a challenge trying to get students to be better listeners. They hear but they don't listen. I have heard it said that hearing, is knowing that the music is playing, but listening is knowing what the words are saying.

Listening is becoming a dying art, I believe, as is reading. I often watch or listen to talk shows, and what I find weird often times is that all the participants are speaking at the same time, especially if the argument relates to political issues. Who is listening? I wonder. I think we now live in a culture where people just talk at each other. This culture has found its way into the classroom.

Because of this, I am aware that what I say and what students hear are often not in harmony. So, repetition is one of my favorite teaching strategies; repetition in as many forms as possible, in songs, in rhymes, and in stories.

I have to remind myself that perception and interpretation are two factors that act upon what leaves my lips, and what gets into the learner's ears.

I try to be very clear with instructions, because sometimes what is said in class and what students report to parents are horses of a different color, in a manner of speaking.

Because of the misunderstanding of verbal words, I spend much time making sure that I say what my students hear, and what I mean is what they understand.

Based on what is required for effective teaching and learning, the daily classroom routine is steeped in multitasking.

# 5

## Road Blocks

### Talking!

Why was it not taught in my teacher training education that constant talking was such an integral part of teaching. My advice to anyone wishing to become a teacher is this. If you don't like talking constantly, consider some other profession.

I talk from the moment students enter the class in the mornings until the last one leaves in the afternoon. It is scandalous the number of times I have to repeat the phrase "stop talking" during a lesson, because of the interruptions or distractions it often causes. Talking is good, but there are times when silence and listening are required.

Talking to students all day is not only limited to the classroom. On the days when snack or lunch duties have to be carried out, the talking is multiplied. These duties are performed either in the upper or lower school eating areas. No matter where you are stationed, at least half of the school population has to be supervised through constant talking.

"Sit down, eat your food!"

"Don't speak with your mouth full"

"Stop fighting!"

"There is just too much noise!"

"Walk, don't run."

When I get home after school I have no desire to talk. My wife is not a happy camper, but I can't help it. I am so talked out. Talking saps energy and in addition to that, there's the standing and moving around the class during instruction time. Teaching is tough, physically and vocally. My advice to teachers, eat right, exercise and take your vitamins if you hope to survive.

## Forgetfulness!

"Gee! I forget"

If I was given a dollar the number of times students use that expression, I would be rich! How easily the words, "I forget" slide off their tongues? Some don't even bother to try thinking before they fire this expression. It appears that it is too painful to think.

'Atom is the smallest part of matter.' This is the focal point of the science lesson and is repeated many times during the forty minutes session...

Recapping at the end of the lesson;

"Could you please tell me what you know about an atom?"

"Who me?"

"Yes you"

"An atom is …. An atom is…. Gee I figet"

Stressed!

"Forget! How could you forget, I just finish …………… what is wrong with you?"

"Calm yourself," the inner voice chips in, "lest you say something that you may regret, or worse, something that might scar."

*Deep breath…*I try to be very careful and mindful of what I say to my students, no matter the situation. I try very hard not to reprimand negatively. A quote from mother Theresa comes to mind.

"When the words end, the echo continues." Teaching is about building up not tearing down. Students should never be corrected in a negative way.

## Organize

"Why is your area so untidy?"

"Pick up the papers you dropped on the floor" "Keep your area clean"

"How many times must you be told to keep these notebooks on the counter in a neat pile?"

*Is it in their nature to be disorganized?* I wonder, *or do they bring that from home?*

It is now nearing the end of the second term and students have not quite assimilated the rules of organization in the classroom. One rule of organization is that all books and supplies must be stacked neatly on each person's desk before going out for snack or lunch. There is never a time when this rule is carried out one hundred percent, unless, a reminder is given.

One habit that irritates me the most, is when the class is settled and working quietly, then someone breaks the calm by sliding out of their chair and starts heading to where the school bags are stacked.

"Where are you going? You got no permission to be out of your seat." "I am going to get my pen out of my bag."

"Get your pen? What were you supposed to do this mornings when you got in class?"

"Unpack my bag and have everything ready for working." "Thank you, so why was that not done?" "I forget"

That word again.

The main word in their vocabulary.

## Following Instructions

One of the deadliest sins committed by students is not following instructions. I am convinced that they interpret following instructions, to mean 'do as I feel', or at least a part of what was instructed. There is a chronic problem with following instructions, orally or written.

"The instruction asks for you to circle the correct answer, why have you underlined?"

"I don't know, but ain't that the right answer?" *Groan!*

"Please follow the instruction, thank you."

When written instructions are given, and if they appear to be similar to ones they have seen before, chances are that many will not read the complete instruction. They would rather assume that they already know what is being asked. As a result, an incorrect answer will be given.

If instructions ask for more than one response, usually the students will do the first part and overlook the rest.

"Write the numbers in order from least to greatest, then subtract the smallest number from the greatest number." Many times students will do the first part of the problem and ignore the second part. When asked why, the response is, "I didn't see that!"

Translation, "I did not read that part."

The habit of students not reading and following instructions carefully affects their performance.

Writing and good study habits are two areas I have yet to tackle. The road ahead is still an uphill climb.

I refer to these habits as road blocks. They are some of the bad habits students develop that can and will hinder learning. These habits need to be weeded out of students' mode of operation. If not, learning will be handicapped by them. Despite all the difficulties of re-training, progress has been made; but not without considerable talking and reminding.

# 6

## Creative Teaching

Teaching requires uncommon dedication. It is a balancing act of weekly lesson planning and personal endeavors. It takes a considerable amount of time to prepare for instructions, It involves writing tests and exams, planning projects, planning field trips, evaluating, grading, writing reports, and record keeping. These items and more are always on my agenda.

In all of this, creativity is needed as things don't always go as planned. I find, however, that the education system is not balanced enough. Some subjects are more esteemed than others, and the opportunity for the child to explore all of their potential is not given equal importance. There are some crucial components that the system lacks, due to insufficient funding. However, the one that I would like to see develop in our system, that is not in place presently, is a vibrant visual and performing arts program.

Any education system with this component added, I believe, would provide for students a more rounded education. I find it very difficult to teach just bound to a curriculum. I would simply die if I were not allowed to find space in the curriculum and in the students' school life to immerse them in creative activities like singing, dancing, acting, or reciting.

It is a passion of mine to expose students to the performing arts, and even have them compete in local festival competitions. The objective is not for them to win, though that would be a source of pride and joy, but the objective is for them to be in a different learning environment. It is an opportunity to be exposed, and gain experiences that the classroom simply cannot provide. I want them also to enjoy the experience of being in a competition, and hope that it becomes a cheerful spot in their lives for years to come.

Many aspects of students' personalities, hidden abilities and learning difficulties, are often exposed through the performing arts. I have discovered, too, that some of their learning problems can also be remedied through the performing arts. I also use the performing arts to motivate students to do well in the other subject areas.

The performing arts time is like a treat that my class looks forward to. In order to participate though, students must complete their work on time, correctly and neatly. Because of the joy they get from the performing arts activities, every child tries to do what is necessary to get the opportunity to take part.

"Patter cake, Patter cake, baker's man You cannot bake a cake as fast as you can Unless you understand what you reading man"

"Very good, however you need to say it with more energy, and do these actions along with the words."

I demonstrate the actions.

The students are delighted and energized as we work on the presentation which the class is going to use to promote the new reading program throughout the school. From Nursery to Grade Twelve, the push is to get the entire school collectively reading a total of twenty thousand books before the end of the school year.

"Now let us continue."

"Reading, reading, yes, yes, yes
Don't you know that we are the best?
We reading here, we reading there
We even reading in the atmosphere
Hurrah!"

The extent of the value of the performing arts in the classroom did not dawn on me until one fateful phone call changed everything.

Some years ago, I received a call 'out of the blue', so to speak. To my surprise it was a former student.

"Sir," the voice on the other end of the line said in a fine British accent. "I've been trying over the years to reach you." She identified herself with Reverend attached to her name. I remembered her as being one of the first groups of students I taught after leaving college.

The memory of her came back vividly to my mind. When she was in my class, she had just migrated to the island from Britain where she was born.

"Sir," she continued, "you must come to England to see what I am doing." From our conversation I learned that she was working with children who were 'drop outs' who were told that they could not learn and were from backgrounds that robbed them of self esteem and motivation. She said, she had taught the children what I had taught her when she was in my class. It included the folk songs, the dance, and the drama. She continued explaining in a state of excitement.

"Sir, I will never forget those English classes, when you read poems and stories to us and had us acting and singing."

As we continued the conversation I began to re-live those times, so precious. She told me how she had taken her students all over her country and to other countries to perform, and how there was a big 'to do' about them in the media. She said that through her artistic program the self esteem of her students had grown, and how many of them had gone on to be doctors and lawyers and other professionals which made her very proud.

I was silent on my end of the phone, just listening to her story.

"Sir, what I am today and what I do are because of you. In all the things you taught us, you taught us how to love. You must come here and share in this experience."

Tears welled up in my eyes. When I started out as a young teacher I had no clue. All I knew was that I wanted my students to be happy learning. I was humbled to know that I was a positive influence in this student's life. I pray that before I die that God will bless me with the opportunity to honor her request.

# 7

## *Reflections*

I write this chapter with bated breath, unsure of what I will unearth as I wander down memory lane. Reflecting on my own experiences as a child in school, the memories began flowing from my thoughts like oil from a drum, cascading down in lucid thoughts that made everything seemed like yesterday.

Number Twenty-Two Belmore Lane, was where my childhood recollections began. I was not born there, but that was where I was nurtured until age twelve, when my mother moved my brother and I to our own home.

My first school was Father Dawkins' Infant School which, today, would be regarded as kindergarten. It was situated at the opposite end of the lane I lived on. I was at number twenty-two and he lived at number five. Father

Dawkins' school maybe had, at most, twenty children and it was an unconventional school. The school consisted of two long wooden benches placed outside in the yard near his two roomed house.

Father Dawkins was old, had a full grey beard and was a pipe smoker. He had no desk, but sat on a wooden chair in front of us. He did more sleeping than teaching. There was no chalk board. We wrote on slates. My fondest memories of that school was the frolicking time we use to have as little children reciting our times table. We would hug each other around the shoulders sitting in a line on that hard bench rocking back and forth rhythmically, screaming the tables at the top of our lungs.

We also had fun making clay people on those occasions when the clay under our feet was wet. I can't remember it raining though, not enough to prevent us from attending school. Though we were outside all day, the sun did not bother us because the area was heavily shaded by trees in our 'schoolyard' as well as those in the neighboring yard.

A question comes to mind as I look back, where did we go when we wanted to use the rest room? There was none, I remember we used to drink water from a pipe standing near the entrance of the yard. Our benches were only a few feet away from it. What did we do when we wanted to use the toilet I wonder? We were little kids and there must have been necessity for such facilities.

All I remembered about my first school was that learning was fun, though I don't remember learning anything in particular. I don't even remember learning to spell my name, I wondered how I did it though, because my entire name is made up of twenty-four letters. I don't even remember learning to read. I just knew I read. I can still remember some words from my first reading book, *"The Royal Reader"*.

'Mr. Joe builds a house Miss Tibbs, Mother Hen.......'

How I got to and from school in those days without any adult supervision is still a mystery to me. All I remember is that I used to walk to and from school with a little girl my age who lived where I lived. I never remember my mother taking me, because she had to be at work before my school even started.

When I began and when I left Father Dawkins Infant School, I really didn't know. But I can remember vividly when I started attending a government primary school. It overwhelmed me. If overcrowding was a disease I would have died instantly.

The school was about ten miles from home. I got there by a school bus. My first day was the worst day of my young life; I thought I was going to die. My mother did not take me to school, not only because of time, but also because of the distance. I was placed in the charge of a girl who had completed her schooling at that school but was working there as a monitor or teacher's aide.

The place where we waited for the school bus was swarming with other children, all in the same uniform. When the bus arrived, it was already bursting at the seams; I wondered where all the children on the outside were going to fit. But fit they did. I was forced into the bus with no effort of my own. Inside, my feet did not even touch the floor of the bus; I was suspended in mid-air by the press of the larger bodies around me. I gasped for air, I could not breathe. It was hot and dark. The bodies of the bigger children eclipsed the light from outside. I cried and gasped for air all the way to my new school. It was a horrendous experience that I dreaded every day until I was big enough to manage for myself.

My primary school days were the best days of my life in spite of the horrible bus experience, which passed like everything else. They were like days of wine and roses. There were no formalities about my first day at primary school, I don't remember any registration, no introduction, no welcome, I was just placed in the infant section of the school, which was located in a side-less shed in a space across from the main school buildings.

I fell in love the first day I was put in that class, with the most beautiful brown skinned little girl I had ever laid eyes on. Her hair was soft with shades of black and brown and was combed in pig tails which reached the middle of her back. She was so petite and quiet.

I was so in love that I could not speak. I don't believe I learned anything in infant class that year. Every day I went to school, I could not wait to see her; I just daydreamed the hours away. I don't think she ever noticed me or knew me. She was from an upper class family; I was from the other end.

Soon, I began to move up the ranks. Learning was so effortless to me; I was always in the top stream. I had many friends. The girl who I was so in love with in infant class was still in the school, but she became lost in the mix as I became more and more socialized in the school environment.

The school was situated almost out in the country. The landscape was a mixture of low hills and shallow valleys. The landscape was what I enjoyed most about the school. When it was break time, my friends and I would dash off wildly up the hills down into the valleys and through the bushes playing cowboys and Indians or police and thieves.

Nothing could compare to the feeling of free abandon in this place. We played every chance we got. When I got home my uniform would be covered with red dirt, the color of the soil of the school yard. My mother would complain every Saturday when she washed my school uniform.

The greatest excitement for my friends and I during our play time was to sneak away to a place where we were forbidden to go. It was a dangerous place, because some unfortunate students had lost their lives there. For us, despite the danger, it was a place of adventure. It was the river, situated at the bottom of one of the valleys.

The river was especially dangerous during the rainy seasons, when the flood waters were gushing at an incredible speed and overflowed its banks. That did not matter to us, it only intensified our excitement.

It was during these times that children were apt to lose their lives by drowning because they would be tempted to go in the flood waters to retrieve coconuts, ripe bananas or other tempting fruits that the river would wash down from the farms on the sides of the mountains. I am glad that none of my friends or I ever suffered that fate.

Though my life at this school permeated with laughter and fun, I can vividly remember my most embarrassing moment. It was not an incident that happened by accident, but one which I orchestrated myself.

It was common place for many students to come to school barefooted. I don't know how those children felt, or how other students treated them. I knew it never meant a 'hill of beans' to me.

Fridays were very informal days. Not many children attend school on Fridays. This was a market day, and many of the students' parents had small farms, so on Fridays they went with their parents to sell produce. Because the school's population was drastically reduced on Fridays, hardly any school work was done. This was usually the time for games, arts and craft and whatever else took the teacher's fancy. I remember some Fridays making flower pots out of tin cans or making door mats out of crocus sacks.

One such Friday I decided within myself to go to school bare feet. I asked my mother if I could and she allowed me to. That Friday morning, I greased my feet liberally with coconut oil, like I knew the bare footed children did. I was fine until about mid day when I encountered the love of my life. The girl I loved since been in infant class.

I think that was probably the first time she ever looked at me. She said nothing, just looked. I didn't know what I read in her eyes, but I saw something. I never felt so small and insignificant in my life. I wanted the earth to open and swallow me.

For the rest of the day I stayed indoors sulking. From that day I swore I would never go to school barefooted again.

I was in Junior Four when the government built a new school for us. It was bigger and better than the old school. I suppose the old school had become too overcrowded. The new school also cut the journey to school by about two miles.

The opening of the new school was set to coincide with the Country's celebration of independence from England. I can still feel the thrill and see the hot sweating bodies of the army of students and teachers marching two miles in the hot sun to our new location. We waved miniature flags of our new independent country, and we were all supplied with souvenirs cups, notebooks, and pencils, engraved with the coat of arms, and the date of our independence.

I did not understand the pride that people felt then as citizens of an independent country. All I knew was that I felt overjoyed to be occupying a brand new school. Later, I boasted about being among the first set of students to be housed in the school at such an historic moment in time.

In the new school I skipped a grade. I was never told why. All I knew was that at the beginning of the new school year, I went into Junior Four as was expected, but by mid morning of that day I was pulled out, kicking and screaming, to Junior Five.

This was the Common Entrance Class. I cried my little heart out. No one explained to me why I had been moved, leaving my friends behind. I was scared of the teacher I was going to meet. She was an excellent teacher, but vicious, especially when it came to beatings. She was so vicious the students nicknamed her 'HOG.' It was in Junior Five that the word study became a part of my vocabulary and a part of my life.

The unique thing I noticed about this class was that it appeared to be an elite private school within a public school. Later I understood why it was that way. More than ninety percent of the students' parents were professionals; doctors, lawyers, teachers, bankers, nurses and so on.

For the first time I realized I was rubbing shoulders with the 'cream of the crop.' I had to conform; I had to develop ambition, I had to compete, I had to study, I had to attend extra lessons to prepare for the Common Entrance Examination to get me into high school.

I soon found my footing, especially when I found a soul mate, my best friend. How we became friends, I can't remember. Maybe it was because we sat together at the same desk.

His father was a well known businessman in town. He was a privileged boy, I was not, but as they say opposites attract.

Every time I remember him, I remember a funny experience, though it was very painful at the time. We were in extra lessons class one afternoon after school. The class was conducted by our homeroom teacher, the vicious one, 'HOG.' She gave us a list of words, and we were to find opposite words to match each one.

Included in the list was the word 'selfish.' I did not know what the opposite for that word was so I asked my friend. He told me 'buyfish.' I raised my hand and when asked by the teacher what the opposite of 'selfish' was, I answered boldly 'buyfish.' I will never forget the beating I got.

My friend was not trying to be smart. He considered the word to be 'sell fish' so logically the answer should be 'buy fish.' To this day, the incident still amuses me.

When the Common Entrance Examination results came out my best friend and I parted company. We were placed in different secondary schools. His school was in the town where we lived and my school was nearly twenty miles away in the city. I believed I suffered psychological damage from the sudden parting. We never saw each other again. I don't know if he was affected by the separation, but

I was. Since that day I never developed close friendships with anyone like I had with him.

High school days were incomparable to my primary years. I was now going to school in the city. Getting up at five a.m., when it was still dark, to catch the six o' clock bus to be at school on time, was a task.

I remember my first day of high school; I wore short khaki pants to school. Some first year boys like myself, who were city boys, confronted me in the boys' bathroom. They told me in no uncertain manner, not to come back to school the next day with my knees uncovered. I went home that evening crying to my mother to buy me long pants.

I was now exposed to new way of life. There were more distractions. A number of times I would allow myself to cut school and go to the mid-day movies with my friends. Other times, I would jump over the back wall of the school and go with them to the Chinese grocery shop to purchase and steal food. We had no thoughts of the dangers we were putting ourselves in, and the disgrace that would be brought upon our parents if we were caught.

My mother had no idea what I did when I left home to go to school every day. I am sure it was her prayers that kept me. In the mornings before the first bell rang, my friends, who came to school early and I would congregate under the branching shady tree near the school gate and talk all kinds of foolish adolescence stuff, mostly about girls and sports. I was beginning to have interest in many girls.

Summer time was always the best time of my high school days. Why? Because I lived near a canal, and during the summer break my friends and my brother's friends would all hang out at our house.

They would start arriving after they knew our mother had left for work. The house would be filled with young boys and sometimes girls, bad combination; especially when there was no adult supervision around. We would swim in the canal all day, cook, and eat anything we could find or purchase. My brother and I had the frantic responsibility of putting the house back in order when our friends left. Our mother kept a spotless house, so everything had to be carefully put back into place before she got home. That was a task.

There are many differences between my school days and now. The biggest difference, I think, between then and now is that in my days we got to be children longer, and we were not bombarded with so many negative distractions like the students of today.

In today's education system there are so many restrictions and laws; teachers cannot touch students and there is a 'standoffish attitude.' Some parents and students don't respect teachers, and some teachers don't care enough. Whatever the reasons are, I wish education could return to a time of trusting and genuine care.

# 8

## *Ahead*

Where I go from here is already ordained. I am just continuing the purpose for which I was born. Where my destiny leads, I believe, will be on a road less travelled.

*"All the world's a stage*
*And all the men and women merely players:*
*They have their exits and their entrances;*
*And one man in his time plays many parts…"*
William Shakespeare-(*As You Like It*)

I have had my share of parts, some were good some were bad but the lessons were invaluable. I may or may not continue in the teaching profession; but, come what may, I will still be a teacher at heart. What students need a lot of today are love, hope, and inspiration. Education must cultivate these. If I were to sum up my feelings as a teacher I would borrow the words of this prayer;

*'Teach us Good Lord*
*To serve you as you deserve*
*To give and not to count the cost*
*To fight and not heed the wounds*
*To toil and not seek for rest*
*To labor and not ask for any reward*
*Except that of knowing that we do your will'*
*Amen.*

I remember when I first heard this prayer said by the students in school. It really bothered me. I was bothered by it because I felt that whoever picked it as the school's prayer did so because they wanted to send a message to the staff. Were they serious? Did they honestly believe that anyone could be so selfless? Was that the way they expected teachers to be?

Over the years I rolled my eyes every time the prayer was said. But I also found myself reflecting on it. Then the revelation came, not suddenly, but like the rising sun illuminating the darkness in my heart.

It was as if a voice asked, "How can you be truly a committed, dedicated, and loving teacher and be bothered by the words of that simple prayer?" Then It dawned on me, if I embrace that prayer as part of my philosophy as a teacher, then for sure I would be walking in the footsteps of Jesus; the greatest teacher of all.

I realize that education is a gift given to me to use and to change lives in a positive way. Each life that is changed will impact the world, creating a ripple effect that will continue forever!

Email address : jike1353@gmail.com

www.ingramcontent.com/pod-product-compliance
Lightning Source LLC
Chambersburg PA
CBHW022122050726
47591CB00002B/901